The Paths
I Must Walk

Written in four parts by
Duane Beatty.

PublishAmerica
Baltimore

ISBN: 1-60672-755-9
PUBLISHED BY PUBLISHAMERICA, LLLP
www.publishamerica.com
Baltimore

Printed in the United States of America

To Mom,

Though yours has ended,
know that you have led us all down the right path.

Acknowledgments

Though there are so many that I would like to thank personally here, the page just isn't long enough. So for those not listed, know that I know who you are and that each of you has inspired me in some way or another.

That said, I would like to thank my family who has always stood by me no matter what path I walked. Dad, Curt, Allayna and Deanna, I'm glad to be home.

To all the teachers that I have had in my life, both in and out of class or school, you bring inspiration to all of us. Whether you know it or not, we do. Thank you.

I would also like to thank a few friends who have pushed me to achieve a life long dream and who have helped me along the path in their own ways. Wendy, Chris, Joan, Todd, Alvaro, Kevin, Donna and of course Tracy (Margarite Silvia Maria)...you are my inspiration.

Last, but not least, all of the people at Publish America that have helped me put this book together to share with the World.

We all have a path we must walk...walk on!

The Paths I Must Walk

Written in four parts by
Duane Beatty

THE MAIN PATH

The Paths I Must Walk

After each night, I wake
To greet the morning's sun
Rising high to shine upon
All the paths I must walk.

Quite unlike the north star
On the clearest of dark nights
Leading the way in my dreams
To the paths I must walk,

The waking sun allows
No direction to my steps
Showing no favor to one
Of the paths I must walk.

My choices appearing
So equal on the surface
Making no signs clear to me
For the paths I must walk,

Yet each day continues
Turning left or turning right.
I am simply following
The paths I must walk.

Reflections in a
Fitting Room Mirror

As I carried the shirt into the room
And was surrounded by four walls of glass,
A thought struck me so convincingly
I nearly buckled beneath its pressure.

Four endless rows of soldier-like men
Identical
Radiating from me
Like the streets at a four-way intersection
Each of these men
An exact replica of myself
Fading ever so slightly
As his distance from me lengthened.

In that instant, I realized
That each of these men
Was an event in my life—a memory
Fading as time went on.

Those with their backs to me
I dared not face.
While those to my sides
Could be seen through sidelong glances.

But the thought which hit hardest
Was of those who stared back at me
These were the memories most clearly seen—
These were the good times.

The Angel of Chris

It's not a mistype,
The name of Chris
But an honorarium
In the midst of bliss.

From the name of Christ
Comes the name of Chris
And it's through these words
I show the gist.

For she's an angel
Among the midst of men
A tool of God
And of love, Amen.

She tends her sorrows
With a love so brave
And of herself
Her love she gave.

With trouble of a love
In her heart so deep
It's the love of friends
She'll always keep.

To think of others
Is what she feels
And not what she wants
Her heart appeals.

From St. Theresa
She has learned
That love of friend
Is what she's earned.

There will never be
A way to repay
The love she gives
Each and every day.

And it's with these words
And all I miss
You'll come to know
The Angel of Chris.

Celebrate My Emotion

Rainy days spent in solitude,
Sunny days filled with gratitude.
Emotions constantly changing,
High and low they're ranging.

Singing freely in the morn,
Yet another emotion born.
Boredom in the afternoon,
Anxiety rising with the moon.

Seldom does a day go by,
Where no emotions tear my eye.
Water on my face racing down,
Whether into smile or into frown.

Without emotions, I couldn't live,
A purpose to my life they give.
Rolling through like waves on the ocean,
I live to celebrate my emotion.

A Story to Tell

There is always a story to tell,
A story of the future or the past.
A story on which our minds will dwell.

Like the story of the star that fell,
Falling to the earth so fast.
There is always a story to tell.

Or the story of a fiery hell,
All other evil it has surpassed.
A story on which our minds will dwell.

And the story of the wishing well,
Forever will our wishes last.
There is always a story to tell.

A story of a great magic bell,
Ringing atop a towering mast.
A story on which our minds will dwell.

Stories can be like a witches spell,
For on these stories our lives are cast.
There is always a story to tell,
A story on which our minds will dwell.

Revelation

As I sat in the golden dawn,
Knowing it would soon be gone,
I watched my life go by,
Bringing one small tear to my eye.

The beauty of colors spreading,
Sure of where my fate was heading.
Toward that stronger pull;
I'm glad my life was full.

Sunshine on the pond glistening,
Only the wildlife listening,
As I weep for each day passed,
For today will be my last.

I feel my energy drain,
Now the clouds will pour their rain.
My spirit shall soon be free,
Rising higher than any tree.

The final storm begins to rise,
And I lie down to close my eyes.
The end is so very near,
My beating heart is all I hear.

With a final exhalation,
I see the revelation.
The light is pure and bright,
What a beautiful sight.

Thinking Of...

Rolling fields of amber wheat,
(Wars)
Waves lapping at my feet,
(Bars)
Blue skies up above,
(Cars)
These are what I'm thinking of.

The beauty in butterflies,
(Stain)
Sunshine glistening in your eyes,
(Rain)
The pleasure of true love,
(Pain)
These are what I'm thinking of.

The smell of steaks on the grill,
(Deceit)
The roaring rollercoaster thrill,
(Conceit)
Clothes that fit you like a glove,
(Receipt)
What am I really thinking of?

Ignorance

Ignorance more commonly shown,
Is intelligence unknown?
Why won't anyone look,
Not at the cover, but the book?

Is it so hard to understand,
That we all walk hand in hand?
Who cares what color, creed, or race?
The problems are the same we face.

Gays or straights or bi's,
Any shape, any size.
All children in God's mind,
A place in life we hope to find.

Old-fashioned are everyone's views,
That's apparent by the news.
Everyone quick to criticize,
Everyone living lies.

How easy life would be,
Our hearts and minds set free.
If it weren't for our stance,
To maintain our ignorance.

What Does Friendship Mean

What does friendship mean,
When two people feel so close?
Is it the tenderness they feel,
When they hear each others voice?

Is it the compassion they feel,
When something troubles the other?
Or the help they can give,
When the other is in need?

Is it knowing what is meant,
When no words are spoken?
Or the admiration felt,
When the other rises above the rest?

It is this and so much more,
In my definition of friendship.
And all of this I have come to know,
By being able to call you friend.

What Can I Do for You

What can I do for you
To help ease the pain?
Tell you she's better off,
And has everything to gain?

Those words feel empty,
They're what everyone will say.
What I feel is much deeper,
And the feeling will stay.

Because when you hurt so much,
I feel it in my soul.
And helping you feel better,
Will help me feel whole.

Maybe in words I can't express,
What you want to hear,
But when you need a special hug,
I will always be near.

Holocaust

See the terror in their eyes
When they suddenly realize
That life as they have seen
Has turned so dark and mean.

One small button beautifully red,
Is turning everyones weary head,
One great flash of bright pure white
Warns everyone of their plight.

Missiles launched from submarines
Silent flying killing machines.
Quiet until they reach the ground,
Only then do they make their sound.

People everywhere sick and dying
Nobody cares, no one trying
To find the fault or place the blame
Too busy hiding from the flame.

Is this the future that we see,
The way that life was meant to be?
We should try our damndest, forget the cost,
To prevent this deadly Holocaust!

Work

Six in the morning,
Day in and day out,
Can do no more,
Than make me pout.

Every day is the same,
I can't take it anymore,
Got to work to get paid,
And work is such a chore.

The worst, of course, is when
The sun is shining brightly,
And I am always tempted,
But just close the blinds so tightly.

If only I had a month,
Wouldn't it be grand,
Instead of going to work,
I could lay out in the sand!

Magic

There is always something mystical,
About the magic in the air.
Things don't always seem so physical,
For those who really dare,
To see beyond the normal sense
And show how much they care.
They can't survive without suspense,
Or the thrills they want to share.
So open up your heart to all,
And do what's really fair.
Don't worry about the chance to fall,
'Cause magic's in the air!

Sometimes I Wonder

Sometimes I wonder
What I'm doing here,
Searching for love
That is nowhere near.

Sometimes I wonder
What life has in store,
For someone like me
Will I hurt evermore?

Sometimes I wonder
What will I do,
When I find someone that
Won't remind me of you.

Sometimes I wonder
And then I think why,
'Cause all of this wonder
Won't change the sky.

So now when I wonder
I wonder about me,
I get a strange feeling
That I'll always be free.

Tires on the Edge of Life

The wind flows through my hair
Like the ocean current through seaweed
As I course my way
Down the snakelike highway
Headed for a future
I no longer understand.

Time seems to quicken
As I rev the engine faster
Than its ever revved before
And watch the telephone poles
Pass before me like fence posts
In a neighbor's front yard.

How long can I go on like this
Tempting fate by staring it down
Will the time that I am racing
Catch me in the end
And laugh wildly at me
As it spits dust in my face?

I have been duly warned
By friend and foe alike
Told of experiences they've heard of
Each gruesome in its own way
Is this what lies in store for me
As I drive my tires on the edge of life?

The Wait

The wait
The wait is the impossible thing
Never knowing when
Never knowing how long

The wait
Trying patience in every way
Always in control
Always bending the rules

The wait
Breaking down every will
Keeping suspense high
Keeping nerves on edge

The wait
How long can I go on like this
Biting my nails
Biding my time

The wait
No longer must I wait
It's over
It's done.

Bright Lights

Bright lights and flashing colors
Intensity both real and imaginary
Flowing like electricity
Through endless coils of copper wire.

Snowy patterns and static noise
Lasting long into the night
Yet daybreak brings the sounds of life
To ears so bent on listening.

Our children programmed by the violence
And scared by the horrified screams
While being taught the simpler things
By some large and yellow bird.

All this seems to happen daily
Custom fitted into our routine
And if you've read this carefully
You'll see it on your T.V. screen.

The Excellence of Average

I've often wondered
What turns My life would take
If I were to excel
In at least one thing—

To be the best—
The best poet?!
The best actor?!
Gymnast?! Dancer?!

Why must
Everything be average?
Average Looks
Average intelligence
Average skill

Average looks
Won't make you a star
Average intelligence
Won't get you far
And average skill
Just makes you par

Average is inadequate
Around those who excel
And only better
Than those who are inadequate.

Yet there is one thing
At which I excel
I excel
At being average.

Fishing

Which do I keep?
Which do I throw away?
Do they want to be caught,
Or be the "one that got away?"

Choices such as these
Aren't as easy as they seem;
None of them are perfect
Like the one that's in my dream.

Like a whirlpool my mind is spinning
Confusion pulling me down;
My thoughts shipwrecked inside me
Turning my smile into frown.

And yet there's always a hint of hope
Sending me back out to sea;
To find the one that I can keep
The one that's right for me.

Rehearsal

Bees in and out of their exits
and entrances
Seemingly no purpose behind
their movements.

Each scene the same
Day in, day out
Just different players
different song

Running here, running there
Queen bee yelling orders
"Three steps left, two to the right,
one up, one back, let's go!"

From afar all looks askew
But on opening night
The results are shown
A play is born!

Life Changes

Life changes
Everything rearranges
Some things remembered
Some things not

Family lasts forever
Friends stand together
Life changes
Everything rearranges

Remember the good times
Forget the bad
Try to be happy
Skip the sad

Life changes
Everything rearranges
Some things remembered
Some things not

Communication

Communication
A two way street
There are no wins
There's no defeat

You're right
You're wrong
Feelings are always
And never strong

Communication
A two way street
The crossroads
Are the place to meet

Communication
A two way street
There are no wins
There's no defeat

What Do You Know?

What do you know
When you don't know enough
What do you know
When you do know enough

Is enough enough
Or a state of mind
What do you know
You still have to find

I am, you are, we are
It's a state of the heart
What do you know
To challenge the part

Take the time
To realize
What do you know
I read in your eyes

What do you know
When you don't know enough
What do you know
When you do know enough

How Life Goes By

How life goes by
I often see
What life itself
Has offered me

Memories
I will not lose
Of Life the way
I did not choose

Diving in
The oceans deep
Swimming sharks
And things that creep

Riding in
Life's rodeo
Things that come
And things that go

I'm seeing things
Through childs eye
I've lived my life
How life goes by.

Just Be You

Life is full
of little quirks,
ups and downs
and sideways jerks.

But more imortant
is how you live,
what your heart
can truly give.

The nature of
identity
provides the real
serenity.

For when you're gone
they'll see the goal,
the true nature
of your soul.

Friends are great
and love is true,
but most important
is just be you.

Life Is Art

Wind blowing
through the tree
setting each
tree leaf free.
Falling upon the ground
waiting for
the childs hand found.
Pasted on
the page with glue,
surrounded by
palm prints
red and blue.

To Say Goodbye

What happens today
Is tomorrow's pasts
Realize in full
That nothing lasts

Hardship sells
Relationships due
And all remember
That lives be true

But whether girl
or boyfriend be
Look inward and
Begin to see

That lives are lived
And parents see
That what they give
Is life to be

Nothing lasts forever
Don't even try
There are always times
To say goodbye.

Donna's Song

There Donna sits
At the bar with friends
Having a drink
And making amends.

Waiting for
Her chance to sing
Of broken hearts
And broken wing.

She knows that soon
Her time will come
Microphone in hand
And applause from some.

Not to worry
There's nothing wrong
We're just waiting
For Donnas song.

Who Is She?

Tracy Margarite Silvia Maria
All the names she wants to be
You never know which when or where
Who is she?

Tonight it's Tracy
Brazen and bold
Easy to get away
But hard to hold.

Tomorrow Margarite
Subtle and shy
Blushes at all
And wonders why.

Next is Silvia
Proven and sure
Loving and caring
A heart that's pure

But then is Maria
Flying high on wing
Lifting our hearts
And souls to sing.

Sue's Corner

This isn't your normal
Watering hole,
It's a place to come
And bare your soul.

It's not just a place
To buy a beer,
But a place to find
A sympathetic ear.

It's a simple part
Of the neighborhood
Where everyone's always
Well understood.

So come in, sit down
Belly up to the bar,
No matter how near,
No matter how far.

It's where you find
Friend tried and true,
And we owe it all
To Terri and Sue!

Ole Man Winfield

Ole man Winfield
At Andrea's bar
Always sat with a view
Of the old train car.

Ole man Winfield
Forty years an engineer
Felt the vibe of the tracks
With the bar so near.

Two blocks shy of Courtney
I grew up in the 'hood.
It took a few years
Before I understood.

Ole man Winfield
Forty years an engineer
Died with the vibe of tracks
And the bar so near.

I think of ole man Winfield
My best friends Dad
Watch the trains go by
And I get so sad.

Ole man Winfield
Forty years an engineer
I raise my glass
And I share this beer.

PATHS OF LOVE
LOST AND FOUND

Daddy Saw the Look in Mamma's Eyes

Forty years have gone since high school
But he remembers them so clear
It seems like only yesterday
That he lived his senior year

That's the year he met my Mamma
Nothin' could ever be the same
And in the end it seems he knew
She was bound to take his name

Daddy saw the look in Mamma's eyes
Realized he'd won the prize
New there'd never be another
When Daddy saw the look in Mamma's eyes

Now all those years have come and gone
How did it all go by so fast
Forty years and four kids later
They all said it wouldn't last

It's Just a Matter of Time

Sittin' in our homeroom class
'n' wonderin' what to say
Knowin' what I felt for her
I closed my eyes to pray.

Please come my way
Oh come my way

Took her to the drive-in show
'n' didn't have a clue
Knowin' that I loved her so
What was I to do?

Please come my way
Oh come my way

It's just a matter of time
Things will all come true
It's just a matter of time
To get those eyes of blue

Sittin' in my easy chair
'n' wonderin' what I did
Knowin' what I feel for her
The mother of our kid

She came my way
Oh came my way

Sittin' on my front porch swing
'n' missin' her today
Knowin' what I felt for her
I closed my eyes to pray

She went away
Oh went away

Memories of Yesterdays

Memories of yesterdays,
Brought back in so many ways.
Memories both happy and sad,
Memories both good and bad.

In a world such as ours,
Searching for hours after endless hours.
Meeting people so hollow,
Conversations always shallow.

What happiness overwhelms me,
Exploding fireworks within me.
When finally someone comes along,
Singing more than just a pretty song.

In all these words of prose,
I hope you find more than just a rose.
Realizing what you have meant,
In these past weeks well spent.

I wish you all the best,
As you journey on your quest.
Please do me a favor,
Don't become like all the rest.

There is a specialness inside you,
Making everything you do,
Something very special in so many ways,
Bringing back memories of yesterdays.

Life Goes On

Love like ours has come and gone,
In all the days of Man's past.
And in eternity shall go on,
While people search for the love to last.

Someone will find that love someday,
If I'm lucky, it will be me.
Someone will find a love to stay,
That's when their hearts will be free.

The love I speak of is not mine,
There was a day I thought it would be.
That was when my eyes did shine,
And a heaven I thought there could be.

This song shall cause you no remorse,
But my feelings it truly reveals.
For your life has taken another course,
And my heart still pains, not heals.

That time has left me, just as you did,
But will return again I know.
To you and your love, farewell I bid,
And onward my life shall go.

Remember while on these words you reflect,
And your mind begins to wonder.
Their intent is but to gain your respect,
And forever these thoughts we'll ponder.

Love in Return

All my life I've written,
Of doom and despair.
Writing poems and stories,
Whose intent was to scare.

Always I've written,
To release my aggression.
Using a string of bad luck,
And serious depression.

Using words to express,
The pain I've felt inside.
As love after love,
Ran away to hide.

But things now are changing,
Since you've come along.
My life is looking brighter,
As you help to make me strong.

For as I give my love to you,
There is something that I learn.
Rather than heartbreak,
You give love in return.

And We Make Love

Your soft and loving caresses,
Make my body glow.
Your fingers are heaven sent blesses,
Helping my feelings flow.

Your tender lips brush mine,
And make my body shake.
They taste like sweet red wine,
How much more can I take?

Your body so sleek and slender,
These things are what I think of.
As I bask in your splendor,
And we make love.

Think of You

When my days are long and trying,
And at night I feel like crying.
All I have to do,
Is think of you.

With the weight of the world on my shoulders,
All stepping stones turn to boulders.
Comforts are few,
But I think of you.

When problems are too tough to face,
And I can't seem to find my place.
Time I look back through,
To think of you.

And when all is said and done,
I realize that you're the one.
My heart is always true,
When I think of you.

All of You

What is it that you wish to obtain
From this state I call my life?
Is there something that I will gain,
Something more than pain and strife?

We started with beauty and joy,
Now there seems to be confusion.
My heart is not to be your toy,
But I welcome your intrusion.

Come to me with open arm,
And this relationship will mend.
Love me without the fear of harm,
And know that I will be your friend.

I am willing to give my all to you,
To allow you into my soul.
But I will need all of you,
To make our relationship whole.

I Reached Out

I reached out
And you were there,
Showing how much
You tried to care.

At that point
I took for granted
That our friendship
Was firmly planted.

While in trouble
Your heart was kind,
You helped me out
But I was blind.

For at that time
I did not see
That in your thoughts
You needed me.

I was selfish
When you were there,
And made you think
I didn't care.

Struggling with me
So hard you tried
But now you've left
And I have cried.

So now I'm here
With my self doubt,
You'd be with me,
If I reached out.

Your Love Is What I Need

The distance between us has grown,
But neither of us has moved,
Just thrown around by circumstance,
Yet nothing has been proved.

What is it that I have done,
To make you act this way?
Have I hurt you so badly,
That there's nothing left to say?

I've done some foolish things,
And tried to bury the past,
But as time keeps slipping by,
Memories of these still last.

I'm trying now so desperately,
To find the right way out,
And build again your respect for me,
Before there's too much doubt.

It's something I don't deserve,
But pay particular heed,
While in this stage of rebuilding,
Your love is what I need.

I Paused

During the days schedule full, I paused
And wondered of all the pain I caused
Holding these thoughts in, I tried
But feeling the hurt you felt, I cried.

And as I layed down my head to sleep,
Again these thoughts caused me to weep,
For I knew of no way to heel
The broken heart that's yours to feel.

Ask forgiveness from you, I would,
And explain myself to you, I should.
To step beyond boundaries, I dare,
Trying hard to show you, I care.

While You Were Out

While you were out,
I called on the phone.
But didn't leave a message,
After the tone.

So many thoughts
Went through my mind,
Wondering where you'd been,
What fate would find.

I wanted to find you,
And make you explain,
But that would cause embarrassment
And needless pain.

So I worried myself sick,
While sitting alone,
And kept on trying
To reach you by phone.

But alas you returned,
After running about.
You'll never know the pain I felt,
While you were out.

If I Could Only Sing to You

I'd sing the songs of laughter,
For anything you'd do,
And smile forever after,
If I could only sing to you.

I'd sing the songs of bluebirds,
Folded wings and chests of blue,
Finding all those pretty words,
If I could only sing to you,

I'd sing the songs that you could hear,
And whisper things so true,
Telling you I want you near,
If I could only sing to you,

I'd sing the songs in harmony,
And ask you for your view,
Tell me, would you marry me,
If I could only sing to you?

Love Ready-Made

Love like a river
flows in and out
Ebbing a man's heart
With Truth then doubt.

Why must it always
Hurt this way
Bending to and fro
Like a tree in sway?

Is it really worth
The pain that's felt
A waxen heart
Burnt to melt?

Or is it meant to be
The joyous parade
Marching through life
Ready made?

Precision Indecision

You have asked me what causes this indecision,
And all I can say is "I don't know."
Maybe it's the blood still pouring from the last
incision,
Three years, and I still can't stop the flow.

These questions you ask, I've asked before,
And never have the answers been the same.
Rather than look into my soul's core,
I think of love lost, and who's to blame.

I'm looking deeper since you've come along,
And I'm frightened by what I see.
I try so hard to be so strong,
I can't help but wonder, who will it be?

Someone will get hurt someday,
And I don't think I could bear the pain.
But what if it's turned the other way?
It's hurting you that would drive me insane!

So you see, it is that three year scar,
That causes this indecision,
It's not a lingering love that keeps us ajar,
It's a cut made with a surgeon's precision.

Too Much to Ask

Five years alone or one-night stands
And days of holding faceless hands.

Too afraid to give in to the temptation strain
For loving again and feeling the pain.

Five years in which the heart feels rotten
Pain from the last love all but forgotten.

Five years it's been since feeling satisfied
Years without affection and nights I cried.

And now you walk into my life unaware
Showering affection and heartfelt care.

I fall so easily to your charm
Not wanting to see the possible harm.

Then one night I receive no call
And soon realize my heart must fall.

For just as the others in my past
Your love for me has ended fast.

And I ask myself is it too much
To live one life with a constant touch?

Let's Talk

Talking is what we really need,
To understand each other in turn,
Talking will help nurture the seed.

On all the knowledge we wish to feed,
Its importance we must learn,
Talking is what we really need.

For information I beg and plead,
Before making a commitment stern,
Talking will help nurture the seed.

To the words you say, I take heed,
So there are no bridges for me to burn,
Talking is what we really need.

Some words are like a trusty steed,
For them to flow freely is what we yearn,
Talking will help nurture the seed.

It's with these words we form our creed,
And each other's respect we earn,
Talking is what we really need,
Talking will help nurture the seed.

Dream

You entered my dream last night
Showering my mind with light
Bringing color to my sight

Images so bright and pure
Love, an idea, becoming sure
Edging close like fish to lure

You entered my thoughts today
As I woke and there you lay
Waking you as if to play

Then I saw in your eyes the gleem
And realized that it did seem
You are more than just my dream

Blue Without You

The times we've spent together
have brought happiness to
a darkened area of my life,
filling my heart with the warmth
of my love for you.
Times which seem will last forever
only to be cut short
by the closing of the weekend,
and travels back to our
faraway homes.

And when I'm all alone
in this cold and cruel world
so many miles from your gentle touch,
I think of the smile in your eyes
and the tenderness of your kiss.

And it's then that I realize
how far away you are
and how long it will be
before I hold you in my arms
and shower you with my love.

So I call you on the phone
just to say I love you
and hearing your sweet voice
reminds me that I'm always
blue without you.

Living the Fantasy Alone

Have I been living a fantasy?
A fantasy in which only I can see the magic?
The magic that explodes when we're together?
Have I been living the fantasy alone?

Where are you and why are you there?
Why aren't you here with me?
Making the magic, the fantasy real?
Why haven't you called?

Why haven't you called to leave
At least a piece of magic rope dangling?
Rope to allow me to hang on to my fantasy?
Have I been hanging on to the fantasy alone?

I deserve a call, out of respect,
I deserve to know.
Have you pulled away the magic rope?
Leaving me to fall out of the fantasy?
The fantasy I've been living alone?

Through Love's Eyes

The purest shade of blue
Softly coats the skies
As if painted by an artist
Seeing through love's eyes.

And mountains tall and majestic
Are solid in their stance
Showing all their strength
When seen through love's glance.

The words so softly spoken
Bringing gently flowing tears
Are the sweetest compliment
When heard through love's ears.

And nothing in the world compares
Not all of the beauty in art
Like feelings deep inside
When felt through love's heart.

My Shoulder

Large as a pillow
For you to rest your weary head,
Soft enough to absorb
The tears you will shed.

Strong enough to support
The burdens of your soul,
Deep enough to feel
The pain that you hold.

Always so near
In your time of need,
Giving itself over
To your heartfelt plead.

My shoulder is here
With love enough to share,
When your feelings are low
And you need someone to care.

Our Candles Together

In the dark and weary night of life,
A candle glows steadily in the distance.
You've seen it and can feel its warmth,
If but for a moment on the horizon.

So onward you make your way,
Through the windstorms and the rain,
Whose power has caused the candle to fade
To near darkness and extinction.

And while your candle has faded dim,
There seems no light to show your way.
The steps appearing forward may take you back,
And barriers may keep you from your goal.

But as the candle seems its darkest,
Just call out for me in the black of night,
For I will place my candle next to yours,
And together they will reveal a brighter path.

Broken Wings and Broken Hearts

Gently I picked the young chick up
With soft touches and loving words
And took her home to nurture her
As I'd done with other birds.

For broken were her wing and heart
From the struggle she had seen
To no one could she give her trust
In a world so cruel and mean.

As I mended her wing and heart
I knew what soon would be
Broken wing and heart forgotten
She'd be longing to be free

And as I've done throughout the past
I've sent her on her way
Wouldn't it be nice if
Just one of them would stay.

A FANTASTIC PATH

Caught

Caught on the beach in crazy turmoil,
Picnic shelters crumble like tin foil.
Palm trees bending 'til they crack,
How will I ever get back?

Trash flying through the air,
In amazement, I sit and stare.
In a state of awe, sense I lack,
How will I ever get back?

Rain beating down on my head,
Already several dead.
I don't even have time to pack,
How will I ever get back?

Most creatures have found shelter,
Hiding from this Helter Skelter.
Cars on the highways begin to stack,
How will I ever get back?

Sand in my eyes, I can't see,
The bench flying in front of me.
All I hear is the "Whack!"
I will never get back!

The Lion Rises

This heat is unbearable,
The sweat dripping off my nose.
How long have I been like this?
God only knows.
I'm writing this down,
I can't get back to sleep.
I like writing at night,
A healthy mind I keep.
Maybe I'll become famous,
Writing a night time story.
What is it people want?
Is it something gory?
I dreamt of a hanging on the wall,
Where did that picture go?
It was there when I fell asleep,
Why does it haunt me so?
A harmless picture of a lion,
Part of my collection.
Just a fetish that I have,
Simply an affection.
In my dream, the lion rises,
To attack my sleeping soul.
I run for my life,

Satisfied hunger it's ultimate goal.
This dream that I have,
It's been recurring.
Every horror filled night,
My mind is stirring.
But always the picture is there,
When finally I become awake.
Why is tonight so different?
I feel my life's at stake!
There's a growling in the dark,
Is that picture alive?
My God it's on top of me!
Into darkness I dive.

Shadow

Even in your death,
I get no peace.
Will your hauntings
Never cease?

You nagged me,
My whole life through.
Teasing, taunting
All I'd do.

From my birth.
To an adult,
You followed me,
Like a cult.

I couldn't shake you,
Though I tried.
Many late nights
I cried.

Always persistent
You were,
Stuck in my side
Like a bur.

To get rid of you,
I used a knife.
Cutting away
Your very life.

While dying,
You laugh still.
For it's my blood,
That I spill.

The Machine

The great 2000 has come and gone,
And life has changed forever.
No labor used to get work done,
A computer will switch the lever.

Man, an entity has become,
Shall strive for strength no more.
Physical beauty remembered by some,
But most just see the gore.

With heads bloated by intelligence,
And bodies that look the same.
One notices the ignorance,
And wonders who's to blame.

All children produced in factories,
No longer is sex a pleasure.
Men living in monasteries,
And women too few to measure.

What has caused this turn about,
Is it too clear to be seen?
Is there really no way out?
For we have created...

The Machine.

The Dragons of Lore

Beautiful maidens dressed in white,
All of their faces showing fright,
Too young and naive stepping through that door,
On their way to meet with the dragons of lore.

Nothing to save them from their plight,
Except for the brave and armored knight,
Wandering through the lands to explore,
The darkened caves of the dragons of lore.

When upon a dragon by chance he came,
Breathing its fierce and fiery flame,
He wanted so badly nothing more,
Than to slay the deadly dragons of lore.

The dust has cleared and the duels completed,
And dragons all have been defeated,
Knights saving maidens from the gore,
Of the mighty and terrible dragons of lore.

But alas those maidens live still in fear,
Meeting more frightening things each year,
For even though they'll live nevermore,
There are more dreadful things than the dragons
of lore.

A PATH TO HOLIDAYS AND VACATIONS

Superstition

Shattering mirrors and grains of salt,
Make even the strongest person halt.
On their mind a single recognition—
Superstition.

Itchy palms and bells that ring,
Superstitious axes to swing.
Walking through ladders and precognition—
Superstition.

Black cats crossing in front of you,
Toads and warts, what's a man to do?
Follow through with intuition?
Superstition.

Cracks in sidewalks break you Mother's back,
Eerie hauntings too numerous to stack.
Gold fish fires—only fiction?
Superstition.

Hallow's Eve

Witches and Goblins in yer head,
Sights of frights ye learn to dread.
Knowing of what is still to come,
Yet another jigger of rum.

Tonight ye drink yer soul to leave,
And transport ye past this "Hallow's Eve."
While in its wake ye'll not regret,
Those demons that ye would 'ave met.

For 'tis they who'll make ye loudly rave,
And those around'll call ye knave.
Tongues of the civil continue thrashing,
Thoughts in yer mind commence to crashing.

But no one sees the evil abound,
Save for ye on that lonely mound.
Even the ghosts leave ye for bait,
Fitting ye in that jacket straight.

All Year Round

Outside a blanket covers the land,
While I sit here with pen in hand,
And the smell of pine fills my home,
Making thoughts of holidays roam.

With wood crackling in the fireplace,
Feeling the warm glow on my face,
I think of what giving used to be,
And happiness is what I see.

The Christmas spirit I'm writing of,
The time for joy and worldly love.
Such a short time that we can feel,
What makes our brotherhood so real.

Is this the only season in which we give?
Think of the wonderful way we could live,
If in some way we found,
A way to give all year round.

Luck-O'-the-Blarney

Aye my lads and lasses, gather 'round,
I've a story to tell for sure.
Of a man so lucky that he found,
A pot-o-gold so pure!

While walking through the woods one day,
With nary on his mind,
He chanced upon a Blarney,
Luck surely his to find.

He kissed that stone so gently,
And a stump did place it on,
Then sat back and watched intently,
When soon appeared a Leprechaun!

In his Brogue the man did flatter,
Like with the ladies he'd done so often.
What the man said was not to matter,
For the elf began to soften!

With another line of flattering chat,
The elf was caught offguard,
For the man new his plan was pat,
And the end would not be hard.

He would wait until the time was right,
And sneak up on the elf,
Then grab him up and hold him tight,
To get the truth himself!

When an elf is caught in these lands,
He tells all he knows,
And now the elf was in his hands,
With a final burst of prose.

Never in even all his years,
Had he given it a thought.
The elf could not believe his ears,
For he truly had been caught!

"I'll live up to the legend as is told,"
With a frown said the elf,
"If all you want is the gold,
You'll have it for yourself!"

Vacation

There he lies
Soaking up the sun
Inviting viewers
Ready for the fun

Strangers passing
Staring through unseen eyes
Mouthing words
Of forgotten lies

Words heard before
Taking chances known
With strangers unseen
And promises full blown

Vacations meant
For lives to live
Giving chances
To those who give

Feeling no more
Than what's at hand
Vacation seems
A one night stand

Weekend Away

City contains boredom
Weekend's near
Take the time off
And all is clear

Get away tonight
And tomorrow will show
Not all is gloom
To those who know

That the weekend brings
A life well spent
To those who live
The life hellbent

A weekend away
Will clear the mind
Of the daily stress
Left behind.

Paradise—Palm Springs

Paradise—Palm Springs
Where life springs
Eternal

Boys with tans
Lying in the sun
Abundant.

Bodies galore
Waiting for each other
Sexual.

Paradise—Palm Springs
Where men go to play
External.

Mountain

Tall and majestic
Purple in the dawn
Creating beauty in the sun
Till the mornings gone.

Rough in terrain
Yet smooth to the eye
Rising high and mighty
In the morning sky.

Climbers seem to forget
And attempt to hide
The evils they meet
While climbing the side.

Of the majestic mountain
Sure to hold
Stories of climbers
Long untold.

Also available from PublishAmerica

SHINE AND INSPIRATIONS
by Tiffiney Rochelle Bradley

Shine and Inspirations is a text designed to teach humanity the purpose and role of prayer in everyday life. This book seeks to deepen believers' insights and understanding of how a continual prayer life will serve to strengthen the soul of believers and equip them in remaining encouraged while in the midst of life's stormiest situations.

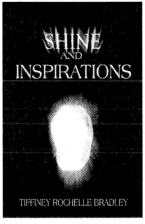

Another book, entitled *Inspirations*, a collection of Christian testimonies, is included. Many of these touching testimonies explain how prayer served to stabilize and/or uplift those who testified out of situations such as HIV, severe physical illnesses, single parenthood, and hunger. Read, enjoy, and forever be inspired as you connect with the Spirit of Christ, which will enable you to Shine.

Paperback, 198 pages
6" x 9"
ISBN 1-4241-8489-4

About the author:

Shine and Inspirations came to life out of my call to serve the Lord, and my passion to help people. Prayer is having an intimate conversation with God. Having a Master's degree in Communications and having served in the field of education has been quite fulfilling, but publishing *Shine and Inspirations* has also been fulfilling, if not more so. What could be more exciting for a communicator and a servant of the Lord than helping others experience a dimension in Christ that I have already experienced.

Available to all bookstores nationwide.
www.publishamerica.com

Also available from PublishAmerica

THE GIRL IN THE PICTURE
by Charles E. Merkel II

Everything is going great for 18-year-old Brian Kitzmiller, who is assigned to a non-combat unit in 1967 Vietnam. His responsibilities include being the outfit's mail clerk, and he soon becomes a welcome face to everyone.

He carries a picture, which he has enlarged then placed above his bunk, of a girl from his hometown whom he really does not know but passes off as his girlfriend. As time goes on, the gorgeous girl becomes the most famous lady in the whole unit and the juicy stories abound. Brian does nothing to stifle this ever-growing myth. In fact, he enjoys his "legendary" status as he has never known anything but loneliness and obscurity back home.

Paperback, 266 pages
6" x 9"
ISBN 1-4241-3047-6

The lid blows off when a cruel skeptic from the same town arrives and Brian's life unravels. Wracked by relentless humiliation and scorn, his decisions from that point become reckless.

About the author:

Charles E. Merkel II grew up in Louisville and Indianapolis, the son of a state engineer inspector and an elementary school teacher. A graduate of the Indiana University School of Journalism and a Vietnam veteran, he has been published in various literary magazines nine times. He has worked as a regional sales manager in the RV industry for twenty-five years.

Available to all bookstores nationwide.
www.publishamerica.com